IMAGE OUT Write

Volume Three

personalpronouns
A Celebration of LGBTQ Writing

Editor Brad Craddock

Cover
Graphic Design Jeffrey Cougler
Image *Juwelia*
Artist Anja Teske
pp Logo Jeffrey Cougler

ISBN: 978-1-312-46195-6

For information about permission to reproduce
selections from this book write to:

274 North Goodman Street, Suite A203
Rochester, NY 14607

Cover Design: Jeffrey Coughler
Cover Artist: Anya Teske
Artwork: *Juwelia*
Project Manager/Editor: Brad Craddock

ImageOut 2014 selected by Steven Farrington, Ryan
Wolfe, Gregory Gerard, & Judy Fuller

ImageOut.Org

ISBN 978-1-312-46195-6
90000

9 781312 461956

Contents

Evelyn Deshane
Closet Trap   8 - 9
Chase Gets Off Youtube   10 - 11
Reincarnation   12 - 13

Tony Leuzzi
After Watching Berger's 'Hawaii'   14 - 15
Home   16 - 17
True   18 - 19

Dale Corvino
Color Me Your Color, Baby   20 - 27

Jes Gonzalez
Sestina From the Margin   28-29
An Aria for Grief   30
The Epic of Switchblade Blake   31 - 34

John McFarland
Everybody Should Be There   35 - 42

Stephen Mead
Coming Out   43 - 44
Pride   45
Dancing   46 - 47

Daisy Cains
First Kiss   48 - 58

Brad Craddock

The Mastectomy   59
Here's Rosemary & a Little Rue   60

Avery Johnstone

While I Was "Out"   61 - 67

Mohammad Seraji

Leap Day   68 - 69
Insanity was Described to Me   70 - 71

Drew Payne

The Third Option   72 - 83

Quinn Powell Gifford

Queen of Hearts   84
Bride to (Never) Be   85 - 86
Rapunzel's Brother   87 - 88

Steven Farrington

Nicola and the Coliseum   89 - 99

Christine Noble

Victoria & Adam   100 - 102

About ImageOut

104 - 105

personal**pro**nouns

Evelyn Deshane

Evelyn Deshane's work has appeared in *The Fieldstone Review*, *Hyacinth Noir*, and *Iris New Fiction*. She is the poetry editor for *Prosaic Magazine*, a regular contributor to *Absynthe Magazine*, and a peer reviewer for *Feral Feminisms*. She lives in Canada.

Closet Trap

My mother has always barricaded her closet,
Afraid of me finding some horrible fashion mistake
from her past.
But what I'm more interested in is history beyond
hemlines.
So I sneak into her room at night
(telling myself I am only cleaning—entirely curious)
And push past the purple ball gowns, cut-off cocktail
dresses,
Pinstriped suits of sensibility 'til I come to her
shoeboxes.

I dig up old photographs, black and white proofs
of a happy existence before I was born.
I find she and my father (before he was gone—
and before she stopped believing in love),
Old parking tickets never paid, pleading notes to get
away,
My name mentioned over and over—and I suddenly
stop.
History is only history for the traitors in the backs of
closets.

But women have secrets, and need to think them
hidden away
among paisley and corduroy. A boy
Young and small, hidden and sometimes sad inside
these photographs
who watched Madonna too young; who grew up and
wanted to be
Joan Jett. That boy was me but not me
He but not he, now trying to write "she"
On form without smiling, like it's the best gift
Or best kept secret in the world. This closet is a trap

Where the old hopes lay and desires stay hidden.
I'm coming out again, wearing different clothing
Leaving behind bad fashion choices
Psychiatric diagnoses and a heap of neurosis
Gender dysphoria and acid washed hopes
Understanding myself and my roots,
My mother and her secrets, like mine,
A little better than before.

Chase (FTM) Gets off YouTube and Goes to a Poetry Slam

I have murdered my twin sister.
She really had it coming.
I wondered from the beginning
if I could escape her. But inside
of mirrors and along my shadows,
she came and whispered my name.
You are a part of me, she said,
and you are mine. We will
never forget each other, I am deep
down in your veins and chromosomes. Then:
I grew weary of the stalking,
of the monitoring,
and the sleepless nights
where she'd wake up beside me.
I decided I would kill her. I filled
the room with exhaust from the car.
I waited and waited,
then realized I needed to shut the garage.
Too exhausting. So I found the razor blades
and lined them all up to spell her name:
Angela, Angela.   What will you do?
I have gotten sick of sharing my room with you.

But even during the night time. Even after
all that I had dreamed, I let the razor blades
fall to the floor and
let my small cuts wash away clean. So maybe
I couldn't kill this girl who had grown up inside of me.
Maybe my hands
couldn't get bigger, or my feet,
or my legs to add an extra inch.
But I could be honest with myself.

I could try and start again,   not
from the beginning, but from this very instant.
Over time, over the shots,
over the surgeries and the pain,
I relearned all I knew about getting dressed.
I learned to respond to a new name.
I go by Chase now.
I like it much better, because now
I know what running means.
The little girl inside of me,
the one I still see in old photos,
tries to reach out and touch this life.
Every wrong name,
every cat scan,
every old license photo. But
I'm okay with the past,
even without getting away with murder.

This has been my confession
to a past life. The interrogation room
is mine and I have always held the key.
I'll walk outside into this new world
and give my sister her last dance.
In therapy, they said:
Let your arms fold around each other,
and allow yourself to desire. To become.
This is the person confessing the final act.

This is the person who I've always meant to be.
A criminal in context,
but now
I am free.

Reincarnation

Wedding and funeral dresses
line the back racks of the store
between two red banners that declare:
  HALF PRICE DAY AT SALVATION ARMY.
  NO RETURNS
  OR EXCHANGES.
I've already lost sight of you
in the mounds of rejected Halloween costumes
                and forgotten crocheted blankets
that used to be on grandmothers' beds.
"Probably now all dead," you say
when you reappear. "I wonder
how many people have died in this clothing?"
It's like limbo, I realize.
The un-baptized souls of unworn
and too-worn clothing are gathering
in dingy bins and touched by sweaty hands.
                        Daily. Hourly.
I wonder what Dante would say about this.
Where he would locate the two of us,
unwed, in this chaos that's now half off.

Being half-priced means we have twice as much work
to do.

And at the end of an hour,
I've convinced you to buy:
                an hour glass full of orange sand,
cowboy boots along with a hunter's cap,
and an old yellow bible with a leather cover –
even though I despise the feel of dead skin
on my hands as I hold it too tightly
and read to you from psalms.

(There was no Dante that I could see
buried amongst the stacks of forgotten words.
 I figure he's forsaken us. I am no Beatrice, after all.)
I am wearing a little boy's soccer shirt
And you a marching band uniform. We are pretending
        To be young again.
To you, this is nothing but "dress up."
But I feel like I'm wearing
more responsibility than that.

Tony Leuzzi

Tony Leuzzi teaches literature and composition at Monroe Community College. In 2012, BOA Editions released Passwords Primeval, Leuzzi's interviews with 20 American Poets. His third book of poems, The Burning Door, was released by Tiger Bark Press in 2014.

After Watching Marco Berger's "Hawaii"

I won't say a word
        about pineapples.
                I will only tell you

when clear water
        pours from an outdoor spigot
                you want it wash over you

the way it washes over
        the pale, chiseled torso
                of a man whose eyes are

the eyes of a child, that when
        he and another man stand
                beneath a giant banyan—

backs lapping the stippled
        light through its branches—
                you forget what you learned

about movement and progress
        and let each word of the sentence
                you were about to utter dissolve

one letter at a time
    while still on the tongue,
        like an unleavened wafer.

And why not? How long
    has it been since you tasted
        wonder and called it silence?

Home

Listen, Jill—I won't
be climbing the hill with you
today. Tomorrow

I plan on writing
a long essay on the word
fetch because I'm not

a Mastiff. Today
however is all about
Bartok's "Sonata"

which I can't play well.
I love to hear András Schiff
pound out those thrilling

last bars thinking yes
the world is terribly real
and complicated.

Today, I will write
a letter in German to
Hansel asking if

he too feels folklore
is weighing him down, forcing
upon him a life

of repetition
and restriction, telling him
who and how to love

and where to draw pails
of fresh well water without
falling or getting

distracted by some
hideous crone promising
parents or cornbread.

Maybe I'll travel.
Viking cruises keeps sending
gaudy envelopes.

Maybe I'll become
a stringer for the local
newspaper, report

fast-breaking stories
about identity theft
and indoor plumbing.

After Pollack, Art
would never be what it was.
I know this because

some of my best friends
are Artists doing big things
in tiny flats. Jill—

my apartment is
small and crawling with vermin.
I'm not coming home.

True

The latest Buzzfeed
quiz—Which 80's pop icon
are you?—says I am

Bon Jovi because
I picked the polka dot swatch
instead of the stripes.

When I retake it—
answering all the questions
the same way except

this time selecting
fluorescent green triangles—
I am Gloria

Estefan without
her city or Sound Machine.
When I retake it

again choosing "Bam!"
instead of "Ka-pow!" as my
favorite comic

strip sound I become
Madonna, which, let's face it,
is the quiz saying

it doesn't know what
the hell I am and wouldn't
I be happier

going back in and
swapping the rainbow flag
for the United

Nations? I would not
mind exchanging "Where's the beef?"
for "Got milk?" but that

isn't one of the
questions. No, I simply don't
think the spider is

cuter than a 4
but if I click 5 there is
hope the result will

feel right, if not true.

Dale Corvino

Dale Corvino has been writing and performing about his history as a sexual outlaw under a pseudonym for the last decade. Under his government name, he's published an account of his family relationship to Marilyn Monroe in Salon.

Color Me Your Color, Baby

I spent my adolescence locked in battle with my little brother. One afternoon riding home from the grocery store in the back seat of mom's car, the battle plays out over control of the airwaves: little brother wants WPLJ (stadium rock), while I want WLIR (Long Island Radio: a local station, progressive, edgier). We strain our slim arms through the gap between the seats to reach the dial, but he's just better at finding his station than I am. Mom just wants us to settle; she turns the dial and lands on a Top Forty station.

They're playing something edgy and fast, crashing guitar licks over a driving beat. It raises my heart rate, and lifts my sweaty butt off the back seat a little, like when you go fast over the Brower Avenue Bridge.

Then I hear a Siren's voice.

Her high-register seduction strikes its target with a direct signal. Little brother reacts with unmediated disgust: "This is disco!" He reaches for the dial; I karate whack his arm and yell, "LEAVE IT!" and give him the crazy eyes.

> *Color me your color, baby.*
> *Color me your car*

I have no idea what this means. I'm not even sure I've heard it right. Maybe because we're riding a '78 Mercury Marquis in the Metallic Blue factory finish—a sharp, optimistic color–I can bury my uncertainty, and accept that the Siren means what she means. I turn myself around and position my head between the rear deck speakers, as the sights roll by out the back window: tract houses, a modernist temple, the bridge over the creek, the jumble of catwalks and docks lining said creek, the last old farm. The deejay announces: "That was Blondie with the hit single, 'Call Me.'"

Some time later, I bike to the discount department store on a busy stretch of Long Beach Road, across from the landfill. The Siren coos into my ear, *ooh-ooh-ooh-ooh-ooh appelle-moi, mon cherie*, and there are a couple of near misses with angry drivers. Stalking the racks of albums, I'm too cowed to ask for help. Another battle rages in the halls of Oceanside High, and here in the TSS record department, I find myself at the front line. I've seen enough 'DISCO SUCKS' t-shirts under the leather jackets of the self-appointed enforcers of social order and musical orthodoxy to know what I'd be in for if word got out. My clique of outsiders already catches hell for liking

New Wave. If you like New Wave, you're a fag. If you like Disco, you're a FAGGOT. Lines have been drawn, and musical genres are on either side, like Berliners.

I can't find Blondie in the album section. There's AC/DC's *Back in Black*, a solid black square with gothic letters; that's what little brother's listening to in his room, he and all the other enforcers. There's *Pretenders*; I've heard "Brass in Pocket" and think it's cool, but then I also think they're British. There's *London Calling* from the Clash, an actual British band, and I've already been branded an anarchist for mock-singing "Lost in the Supermarket" in the supermarket. Wandering those metal racks, doubt overwhelms my mission. Maybe I heard that voice in a dream? I've confused dreams for reality before.

"You know that singer named Blondie?"

Blondie is the name of the whole band, not the lead singer, the die-hards inform me, breathlessly mocking me for my ignorance, while at the same time putting the band in a whole new category of scorn: New Wavers who have given in to faddish disco beats.

"They're sell-outs!"

It's as if they'd committed treason with a synthesizer, and I'm a suspected collaborator. I seek her/them out again at Roosevelt Field, the shopping center built on the airstrip where Lindbergh's transatlantic flight began. I find "Call Me" as a forty-five. I don't dare buy it, I just hold it and stare at the sleeve, a screen print of Debbie Harry, smiling and being cool. I slip the disk out of the sleeve. It says 'Chrysalis' in big letters, a word I don't recognize, even though I've won spelling bees. I'm not reasoning clearly, and I believe I've discovered something precious and rare, possibly both insect and mineral. The butterfly logo should have been a clue, but my heart is racing again; fear of the enforcers, combined with anticipation of getting that rush from the back seat again.

'(Theme from the Paramount Picture *American Gigolo*)' is the subtitle printed below the spindle hole, referring to a movie I'm just too young to see due to its R-rating, 'for sexual content, nudity, violent scenes, cursing, and drug use.' This suggestive phrase, held captive in parentheses, taps me deep in the frontal cranial lobe, like a lobotomy. I really don't know what a *gigolo* is, but just the inferences are enough to fuel my adolescent fantasies of seductive power and ease at negotiating the social world—two attributes I distinctly lack at sixteen.

I don't realize this at the time, because as a dissociative teen boy, I realize very little of consequence. I experienced a major shift in consciousness, brought on by this pop song–a very good pop song, but still. I'll circle back to this moment, that ecstasy in the back seat of that spacious and smooth-rolling vehicle, over and again, for decades. The longing this song instilled in me has bent the trajectory of my existence. It was the song and its connection to the movie, but not the movie itself, remember: I only took the time to watch Paul

Schrader's conflicted, uneven film very recently, on Netflix. At sixteen, I had to supply my own paramount pictures. I never did summon the courage to buy the record, or embrace the band as a fan. Instead I internalized it. "Call Me" became not so much an anthem but a tic, an obsession, like grinding your teeth, or twitching. That driving beat was my adrenaline response; those crashing guitars pulsed at my temples as I stared down at my changing body in the shower, as I dodged the enforcers, as I wandered through suburban nights.

Radio hits are sonic map pins, marking moments in time and geography with a little puncture under a red globe. Debbie Harry's exhortations—her erotic demands, her sultry cooing in three Romance languages, her whispered promises—swirled through my late adolescence. Her voice stilled the hormonal surges, and bleeped out the emotional disorder. Though the vocals confused me on some fronts: was this female voice the inner voice of the gigolo? A rich lady? Who's calling whom, and where did I fit in to this picture? Could this sultry lady voice be an expression of my inner thoughts? Or was I the gigolo-man, whatever that may be—a card cheat, a traveling salesman, an Italian vagabond? Boys can't sing along to Debbie Harry, that's just suspicious.

So I mumble to myself ("Cuh-vah me with kisses bay-bee") in solitary moments, while keeping my guard up against being found out. Still, the song was less fraught and confusing than most things. Strains accompanied me into any situation with erotic promise.

The track levitated me up and out of my flat, insular suburban town. It was an enclave of white ethnics, fugitives from social upheavals and racial strife in Brooklyn. They settled in tract houses built on marshland, forging a cozy détente against the hordes. Did you know that Long Island is a glacial moraine? Meaning a huge glacier dragged its ass over a once-contoured landmass, and left a big rut. I longed to pull myself out of this rut, but as adolescence raged on, I felt it only deepening.

I hadn't always felt this Pleistocene despair: as the first male child in a generation, born to a traditional Italian family, I once favored status. My Italian immigrant family held on to Old-World values through the Sexual Revolution. My immediate family may have looked young and hip, but we were pretty traditional: think Seventies outfits and hairstyles, Fifties moral code and social order. I was treated like a princeling, lavished with indulgences, and favored by my grandma with extra cookies. I had a seat at the big table for Sunday dinners, while little brother and the cousins were banished to a folding thing in the alcove.

Once out in the wider world, I was lost. I was generally unimpressed with my flat, suburban surroundings. I was barely able to form friendships, except with other narcissistic loners. I was overly sensitive, and generally misunderstood. The awkward boy of sixteen in the back of that big blue car heard in those seductive, ethereal vocals a chance to reclaim his power. I'd be restored to my status of privileged charmer. This fugue of affects–that driving beat, those seductive vocals, the suggestive subtitle– instilled an inchoate longing. I wanted to be one who was called, to be an American gigolo. I wouldn't call it an ambition so much as a condition.

Maybe my over-identification with the Blondie/ Gigolo dyad was exacerbated by the fact that I grew up under the spell of another blonde goddess. A candid photo of Marilyn Monroe, who for a brief time was friends with my grandmother, hung in the vestibule of the house I grew up in. Stories of her filled my young mind with star-struck tragedy, so maybe growing up under Marilyn's spectral smile made me that much more susceptible to Debbie Harry's seduction. I followed my Eighties blonde goddess to New York City, backtracking that glacier.

My third year in college, I met a society decorator, an aristocratic Brit of some renown. He was a Romantic and I was his ideal: a rough but pretty Italian youth. He offered me an arrangement. He became my Sugar Daddy, and I was his kept boy for a decade. That would be the gay version of a gigolo. (In fact I think it's the other way around: a gigolo is the straight version of a kept boy.) He took me to his bespoke tailor, where I was fitted for custom suits. We feasted and drank too much in the finest restaurants. We travelled in high style, and I learned to perform the role of outré charmer for his society friends in three romance languages. We visited all the palaces and gardens of Europe, settings he felt I belonged, and I came to agree. It's a story for another day, but suffice it to say, I've been rolled in designer sheets, and I've had enough.

So throughout my twenties, I lived out a (Theme from *American Gigolo*) illusion. Without having seen the movie, the contours of my experience as a kept boy–the wardrobe, the melodrama, the luxury– tracks neatly with those of the protagonist, except, of course, that my Lauren Hutton was a drunken Englishman. Somehow this fate was transmitted to me by that controversial theme song. I took the lyrics–really a gem of pop economy–as an instruction manual, in the absence of any other. Somehow this worked for me, although I can't say I recommend it. I lived through my Sugar Daddy's romantic obsession and all that wine we shared; though they proved fatal to him. Today I know where I'm coming from. That turned-around kid in the back seat found his way.

Jes Gonzalez

Jes, who also goes by Jasper, is a local queer, genderqueer poet who studied Creative Writing and Psychology at SUNY Oswego, and currently works overnights at a call center. They can be spotted with some regularity at Equal Grounds with a set of headphones, notebooks, and pens trying to get some writing done. Heartbreak helps. They also try to read every once in a while, with bashful aplomb.

Sestina From the Margin

this is how to be invisible: let go
of the idea that you've ever been seen
or that what you say will matter.
it helps to embrace being oppressed—
it helps more to live in constant poverty,
which is a dense fog of fear and grey.

walk through your crumbling, concrete grey
neighborhood. it is essential to let go
of old desires. watch the shuffle of poverty
mill around chaotically, and remain unseen
in the tumult. to bare the heart, feel oppressed
by it, as if the air is heavier, with a massive matter.

forget physics to disappear. conceptualize anti matter
and exist in it, between the colors, in the grey
lands of particles. the atom becomes oppressed
with the burden of gravity; it longs to let go
of weak and strong forces. electromagnetism is seen

as only beautiful interference. movement is poverty.
there are different sensations with poverty—

you begin to lose smell, or at least it doesn't matter
as much. your eyes dull at times, seeing
being a luxury. colors clash and wash out to grey.
the drone of sirens, of buses, screaming as they go
by, pulverizes eardrums. the brain is oppressed

by the truth: there are people oppressed
for nationality, for gender expression, for brute poverty.
anxiety stacks on anxiety, fists never letting go
of dreams. no one wants to cease to matter.
but between bills and all that breaks, grey
papers stack up, announcing social stigmas seen

in uncut lawns, rusting trucks, refuse everywhere seen
as common. wading through trash is oppression
on the way to the bus stop. the skies are grey
with rain or smoke or smog. we no longer matter.
i became invisible the moment i let go.

An Aria for Grief

love is not cowardly but you are.
and you
        are not the man
                i thought you were.

perhaps it's unfair i test you through fire
and fire and fire again,
my heart encircled like Brunhilda, on the mountains.

you may be a prince but not a hero—

who is to be blamed for this failure?
the faltering horse, the holocaust path,
the frigid prize who laid on the cool stone bed for you?

        your own weakened countenance,
        which all my strong resolve could not bare?

like Brunhilda i will curse you from my lonely crag,
to feel as i have felt and still feel for you—
bereft, empty in the stone and whipping wind,
all my love turned to ash in your dulcet mouth
        that i will miss,
        as i pray you miss me now.
        in your comfortable castle, with your queen.

        i'm certain you don't. but you will burn.

The Epic of Switchblade Blake

I.

it's fair to say i wasn't always there for you—
          satellites could never faithfully
convey my love.

but what is it about me
that is so easy to leave,
as if there's nothing in my to grieve?

our paper relationship deteriorates
under our damp melodrama.

the knife that cuts the bonds cuts both hands.
the bloody lines across my palms sting
like your fingers,
like salt on the wound.

II.

faithless bitch getting your dick wet—
this is not how love should end,
with your replacement of me telling me
to fuck off.
you're so cowardly you couldn't be bothered
to say it yourself,
or tell me about the new savior/sucker
who found you.

you're like a hermit-crab scuttling from
shell to shell.

i don't need some boy with no spine to speak,
no loyalty and no respect,
to do the killing deed himself,

and instead sending his lover in
to erase my voice from your eyes.

that's fine, i shouldn't be surprised
with what amounts to probable lies.
i have a list of I.O.U.s
for all the shit you said we'd do.

every sweet thing turns to bitter
ashes in my mouth,
like your cum- acrid
and then gone.

III.

how is it that, drunk, i still wade into you
like a nonbeliever into the miracle,
as if you are oasis in my long long desert.
dumbstruck i can only return to the known—
      all of you.

i stumble further into me.
i catch the steady glint
on the horizon.

you become mirage
on my rum-soaked brain,
some image i clutch at for survival's sake.

maybe that's the crueler gesture.

IV.

you changed your name again,
as if you aren't sure of who you are
at any given point—

or perhaps you would rather not know anymore.
or know anyone who knows.

maybe too many broken bonds of men
       you left behind
       have bitterly bitten your name out of
       your sweet skin—
       only to have to spit it out again.

to name a thing is to know it—
and i never knew you at all.
i only held you in my hands for five days.

but i loved you for eight months.
just long enough to carry your baby
until you still-birthed it,
cut the cord to all our dreams
using your scalpel-sharp smile.

i know i share the blame for this abortion-
morbid, i would've held our relationship
in my body until i swelled
with the dead memories decaying my heart,
until i grew sickly with longing.

carrying the evidence of your body inside me
as the only evidence left.

but you changed your name
and i lost my reference to frame you to.
instead, just a vacillating unfamiliarity—
my feeble attempts to end caring
played out as sharp grunts
between clenched teeth.

staccato guttural grief.

V.

we are born with knives in your mouths;
each kiss we kissed was a Brutus.

John McFarland

John McFarland has published short fiction, criticism and essays everywhere from *The Bad Boy Book of Erotic Poetry* to *Cricket* Magazine, as well as in the esteemed anthologies *The Next Parish Over: A Collection of Irish-American Writing* and *The Isherwood Century: Essays on the Life and Work of Christopher Isherwood*. He lives in Seattle, Washington.

Everybody Should Be There

"I sail uncharted waters, I wander hazardous terrain," David murmured as he pressed the buzzer for Apartment 9 on the intercom. Rob and Ted's repeated two a.m. plea, "Oh, come on, everybody should be there, including both sets of in-laws. You'll be in your element," pushed him to accept the invitation from people he barely knew. How could he, though, have said no? He'd just had sex with them all over their apartment, especially on the couch. Now it was nine-thirty, nineteen hours later, and deep into the evening, and from the intercom's speaker came a scream, then dead silence. He tried the entry door. It opened at his touch.

All day long, and even then as he made his way through the hallway and up the stairs to the apartment, he had pictured a small gathering of in-laws and assorted friends punishing each other politely with small talk. At no time had he imagined anything like the din coming from beyond the propped-open door of the apartment. Readying his response of, "I did their couch," in case anybody cared to know how he fit into the picture, he sailed over the threshold.

Inside, the light was cranked up to current standards for surgical suites and all maximum occupancy recommendations had been thrown out the window. People, chattering and hooting, were packed in like cattle.

"Originally headed for Helsinki, I have been rerouted to Cairo," David thought. Looking for a quiet place to regroup, he headed for the bathroom. He locked the door, sat down on the toilet and ran his hands through his hair. The silence and bayou humidity calmed his nerves and he was starting to regain his composure when the shower curtain flew back.

"Holy shit!" he cried, and shot straight up to standing position.

"Did I leave that door unlocked again?" Ted asked and grabbed a towel. "God! I could have ended up receiving everyone and his mother in here. Wouldn't Rob have loved that! Like he's not pissed enough already at me for getting stuck late at work tonight, of all nights."

Ted dropped the towel on the floor and pulled on a pair of fluorescent orange shorts. "I'm the lifeguard on duty, so don't get in over your head,"
he warned David before he opened the door a crack and slid out.

Alone at last in the bathroom, David took a deep breath and glanced over at the photo of the ballet dancer notorious for posing nude and rampant. He was dressed for the party. Pasted on the glass was a leafy tutu that the adventurous could turn back for full effect. Stars know about impact. And entrances. That's why they're stars.

Stepping out into the fray, David made a preliminary pass through the crowd and caught snatches of conversations as he cruised the rooms.

"... Alex claimed it was ..."

"... compared to what I'm used to, no ..."

"... hip-hop's ideal Presidential candidate ..."

"... looked real enough to me ..."

"... twenty-eight, I almost choked ..."

"... maybe London, maybe Mexico ..."

"... one about the Christian stripper ..."

"... in this light ..."

"... he did say large ..."

"... not for me, thank you so very much ..."

He didn't pick up a single clue about who these people were. Nobody he saw looked like an in-law. Could they all be tricks like him?

"You have that hungry look, doll," said a helpful stranger being jostled by the mob. "Food's in the kitchen."

The man was gone before David could say, "Thank you," or ask, "Are you an in-law?"

The crush in the candle-lit kitchen was nothing compared to the population bomb dropped in every other corner of the place. Here he had room to saunter, picking up smallish things from the table: dolmades, quesadillas, wedding almonds, chicken wings. "All of a sudden, my appetite is huge," he thought. He fed it and fed it and fed it.

Luckily for everybody anywhere near him, he had chewed and swallowed everything by the time an arm wrapped around him from behind and delivered a guerrilla Heimlich maneuver.

A husky voice insinuated, "I trust you got your fill of cocktail franks." Then a mouth engulfed David's ear for a good licking.

It was Rob. He was pissed, but not just in the way Ted had predicted.

"Hey, David! Have something more to eat!" he said, wobbling but showing everybody present that he could connect names and faces. "Hey, it's been too long!" he continued, and repeated David's name three times, shaking his head slowly from side to side as if trying to dislodge something pesky from his hair.

"How's every tight inch?" David finally slipped in.

Rob's lolling head moved closer. In a conspiratorial whisper that came out much louder than David would have liked, Rob said, "You're so hot, so fucking hot!"

David shot nervous glances around the kitchen. His first wish was to change the subject. Soon hot, soon cold.

"I ran into Ted when I went into the bathroom," he said. Rob's whole body was swaying as he said, "So fucking hot!" over and over, just millimeters from David's face.

They say you can't have too much honesty. Rob had proved they're wrong even before his endless loop was interrupted by a not-so-old lady outfitted in a lemon-yellow dress, a creation only too familiar to David from Ted's artful turn in it twenty hours earlier.

Rob stared blankly at her. To David, this could be no one but Mama. Standing behind her was a man in neat gray slacks, a forest green shirt and a silver bolo tie. All dressed up, and here he was speechless. Fathers! How silent they fall when faced with their sons!

Towering over everybody, Rob tilted in wider and wider swings. The couple, apparently daredevils, wasn't registering any fear that Sonny-boy might topple and crush them.

"I love your apartment. I love your friends. This has been a lovely party," the woman said to Rob.

Rescued by that line from having his temperature broadcast any longer, David looked at the dirty dishes in the sink and the mucky cigarettes floating extinguished in half-empty plastic cocktail glasses, the absolute dregs. He thought, "Go ahead, Ma, tell the whole truth: that candlelight can't begin to disguise this mess; that a fire warden would shit if he saw this. Deal out the worst, babe, it's way too late to worry about hurt feelings."

She did nothing of the kind. With his own ears, David heard her repeat, "I love your apartment. I love your friends. This has been a lovely party."

There it was, another endlessly repeating conversational line. It had to be genetic.

How many times would it be repeated, he wondered, while Rob strained to speak, eyes narrowed to slits, his head on rattle. "There's a lot of love here," Rob finally managed to mumble.

"You don't have to tell me that, dear," the woman said, wrapping her arms around Rob's waist.

Rob raised his arms and placed one huge hand on each of her tiny shoulders. He drew her in, burying her in his chest.

Whatever she had on her mind and might be trying to say didn't stand a chance of being heard over the thunderous crash from the main part of the apartment. For a moment, all was still. That eerie silence ended with the cry of "Jesus! Fuck!"

While all attention in the kitchen turned to the entry way, Rob said to nobody in particular, "There really is."

Ted appeared at that door. He was wearing the fluorescent orange shorts, but had added a fox stole worn off the shoulders.

Candlelight suited Ted, but he wasn't there for flattering effect. He flipped on the light switch, and rushed to the wall-phone next to the refrigerator. He picked up the handset and punched three buttons.

"Ted!" Rob called. "There is a lot of love here, isn't there? Tell these people just how much."

Although Ted was intent on giving the address and particulars of the emergency over the phone, Rob had his own urgent business. At top volume, he demanded that Ted confirm his inventory of love.

Ted was still on the line, and Rob shakily navigated his way over to him. Reaching out unsteadily, he grabbed hold of the fox stole. He yanked it, pulling it tight against Ted's throat.

"Tell them now, fuckhead! I told you to tell them. Now, do it!" he growled.

Ted didn't tell anybody anything. He wheeled around, phone in hand, to face the wall. Nothing or nobody was going to force him to testify.

Rob fell on Ted, and pulled him to the floor in a clatter. The two of them rolled across the tiles, hollering threats. The dangling phone banged against the wall.

"Muriel," the man in the bolo tie whispered to the woman in the lemon-yellow dress, "I've had my fill of these assholes. I'm going upstairs. If you want to stay, it's your funeral."

He lit out of the kitchen before the woman could answer, argue, or follow. She stood frozen in place as Ted and Rob wrestled on the floor, yelling and pounding at each other. David took her elbow and guided her out of the apartment.

"Thanks for getting me out of there," the woman told David in the outer hallway. "I have to go now. I can get upstairs by myself."

"Upstairs," he thought, "all this talk about upstairs. Aren't these people from out of town?"

"When do you leave for home?" he asked.

The woman gave him a puzzled look. "Home is upstairs," she said dryly.

"Aren't you Rob's mother?"

Her laughter filled the hallway to the rafters, flowed over the balcony and out on to the street. "His mother!" she howled. "God preserve and save us! His mother! Oh, God, no!"

David didn't bother to add, "So, you're not his mother," in case she'd fall down screaming. As it was, she burst into renewed gales of laughter at almost every step she took up the stairs.

David went in the opposite direction, but wasn't laughing himself silly. Downstairs, he opened the front door and left the building. The door closed behind him, a final click. He took a deep breath of the night air. He squared his shoulders, and extended his arms without touching anybody or knocking anything over.

The streetlamp across the way cast a muted orange glow on the parked cars. A window slid open high above him. The quiet in the street at that hour was eerie.

And then all of a sudden, the street went dark for a moment before all the lights, inside and out, flashed back on at once, more illumination everywhere anybody could stand after totally nothing.

"In-laws," he said to himself, "there were no in-laws. I was as much an in-law as anybody else there. And I am outside the law.

Stephen Mead

When not being a creatively-frustrated secretary
employed by a very nice University in NY, Stephen Mead
is a published artist, writer, maker of short collage-films
and poetry/music mp3s. Much can be learned of his
multi-media work by placing his name in any search
engine. His latest release is entitled "Our Spirit Life", a
poetry/art meditation on family heritage, love and the
evanescence of time.

Coming Out

First there's fear, rejection's seed,
the thought that though acceptance has come
for lucky others, if your truth were known,
friends and family would turn.

How easy is denial
or how hard, confrontation?
Is the hidden suspect,
a distant, inward loved one
now, in fact, established as
strange, no concrete relation,
just someone once known?

Oh stone soothsayer, chisel on.
Blow dust. Emit clear flame
taking part in the carving of pulses,
but then, water gentle,
somehow coming out pure.

Tell, convince me it won't flourish,
that, despite toil, I don't flow,
towing roots beneath your hold.

Here is a sound shown strumming
for both listener and speaker.
Is that so unnatural? Does it tarnish,
or is a bond made better by that action, confession?

Emotion is relative with an additional detail of pain.
Will you feel real passion or can you try,
insightfully, to touch reminiscence?

This malleable friendship is an old wick,
incense burning, non-chemical fuel kept alive,
a spoke, its wheel, a film reel-breathing,
slower and slower, human close-up
to close up with, in plain view, suddenly a heart.

How shall it turn out,
attempting to be kind, cautious,
yet bleeding all the while?

Pride

Layers of puff
To keep the neck erect, chin out,
Shoulders quarterback molded &
All this, almost invisible...
Who would like to see the suit
Bleed a little, prove that it's serious,
Show how flesh can become a trade
Off when stripped of the basic
Sustainers: food, roof overhead,
The stereo, the mail box, these small
Luxuries,
Dreams withheld
From the latest trick plopping down
A twenty, perhaps enough for three
Days worth of respite, that untouchable
Interim this throw-away byproduct
Finds while relishing sun on too-soon
Aged skin, a passing pushcart of cantaloupes,
That suburban flourishing windowsill
Glimpsed in a magazine ad
Held tight as armor to his pulse,
The buttoned cuffs
& always immaculately gentle
Public washroom cleansed hands

Dancing

It wasn't a Nureyev, Nijinsky or Baryshnikov,
but purely physical, anonymous as perfection,
a skin we'd love to name.
What can touch identify?
Nothing, I used to think,
bodies blurring in the tango
yet somehow washing up clear, clean, distinct.

Separation defined
everything: the putting back on
of a face like clothes.
These are his shoes, those, his keys,
the essential
break, then retrieval of a fit which
felt true.
I believed that's what was needed, no
sentimental shenanigans of
come, stranger, stay

while I had a function, say, of a shower
stall or confessional. That use too
was self-cleaning, effacement for
the next time with only
scars remembering the first: the ancient gangbang mirage.

You weren't there for that, only
a partner the stage tossed forth & by then
I'd brainwashed myself, poker-faced through it all,
not intimacy, but a business.
Know thyself by holding back.
Change sheets like locations, a creed of extreme
bleaching with paper to catch
everything which fell between...

I was best kept there, but you came inside, kept
coming & no one asked, no one explained that colors
would dance themselves out & continue to dance,
that dancers must give entirely as we do,
learning each new step, choreography by improv
without even paper
to record how lines disappear.

Your skin's torched the notebooks.
In your face I forget pens.
Though every finger scribbles rich as calligraphy,
I lose names, words; I am lost in the finding,
the strange heights which leap, embrace,
& even sleep as gain.

Daisy Cains

Daisy began life as Ian who was in turn a bad barrister, an indifferent teacher, a lazy antique dealer and a nascent novelist. Ian's novel *The Unsinkable Herr Goering,* a comedy set during WW2, was published by The Cassowary Press in 2013. Daisy/Ian's newest novel *Until You Get Caught* will be published in November to coincide with the fortieth anniversary of the Birmingham Bombings. Daisy/Ian increasingly writes as Daisy and also increasingly lives as Daisy.

First Kiss

There are many reasons why I didn't go up to Michelle that night at the school disco and most of them are obvious. To start with I wasn't absolutely sure she felt the same way or if she could even feel the same way, if she was made that way. Then there were the glaring reasons, the ones that grabbed you by the scruff of the neck and screamed 'don't do it!' right in your face, the fact that I was shy, nervous, geeky and bookish whilst she was beautiful, strawberry blonde, slender, elegant and sadly vacuous.

But more that all those reasons it was what had gone before that made me hold. What had happened with Evie made me nervous, and what had happened with Jenny made my hesitate.

Evie with her long blonde hair and long brown legs. Her almost completely flat chest and her pert little nose. The things we could do together, walking around

Chasewater picking wild flowers! If she could come to the Abbey Gardens with us, we would wander through the meadow surrounded by the tiny twinkling flowers of the wild garlic plants bathing in the gentle ransoms aroma before we had to do battle with the evil mulberry tree. Next I could show her my brood of ducklings in the secret pond near the seashore where I would put my fingers inside her Aertex sports shirt and feel the buds of her slowly starting breasts.

I thought these thoughts as I watched Evie on the gymnastics equipment in her Aertex t-shirt and thick navy-blue gym knickers, her pelvis standing proud and the tiny mound in the centre.

Poor Evie who had so little time left.

I doted on her, she had more angles and spiky bits than me, but I adored her, so thin and brittle. I was chunkier, gauche and awkward, she was elegant, a glider, an athlete and a gymnast and I loved her in those thick blue gym knickers, pelvis proud as she did that exercise in gymnastics that I always found impossible, where you lie on your back and push yourself up into a crab shape. I can remember looking at her tiny mound beneath the thick blue cotton.

But she went and died in a car crash and did we get any counseling? Did we? Hell. Nothing at all, it was simply not considered, not necessary, not on the agenda.

I just wanted to talk to someone, but that sort of thing was scoffed at back then. It was something that Americans did, Americans and their shrinks, Woody Allen and spending years and fortunes on therapy. Not necessary. We had our stiff upper lips. I didn't even get to go to the funeral. I wasn't asked. No closure, although the concept of closure was unknown to us as well. Looking back I'm quite pleased not to have gone to the funeral. The thought of her tiny, pretty body heading for the flames, the bones going up in smoke filled me with horror. It still does.

We dealt with it in our own way, on our own, God how I cried. I can still almost cry now when I think of her running, gawky, but fast. She carried less weight than me in the egg and spoon race. We'd read Betjemen to each other, especially 'Myfanwy' and that was all I was left with.

Asking the hole where she'd been: "Were you a hockey girl, tennis or gym?"

We were both tennis girls at heart although I played hockey for the school and she was the gymnast of course. The memory of her blue knickered crab still mesmerized me.

I changed schools very soon after Evie's death and I found Jenny. There she was walking around the outer edge of the all-weather hockey pitch. Jenny, tall with long straight blonde hair, my second and soon to be superior 'Myfanwy' although I had to tweak the 'Myfanwy' stuff because Jenny wasn't a 'hockey, tennis or gym girl.' She was a soccer girl and she he was really rather good and not just at playing the ball. She was equally good at playing the man or even the man's ball. The FA rule banning mixed soccer after the age of eleven saved many a school boy from a severely bruised shin or worse—god, she'd got a kick on her.

Jenny's Dad worked in Africa somewhere and her mom lived out there with him lording it over the natives. Jenny was marooned at the school, lonely and sad whilst everyone else saw their parents at weekends. So when my mother and father arrived to take me to lunch on Sunday I invited Jenny along. I invited her along every subsequent Sunday as well. Those Sundays were fun. We ate real food rather than grey boarding school pap, saw the sights in the area such as they were, and Matt misbehaved constantly for no obvious reason. Mom told us ignore him, 'he was just going through a phase.'

Those Sundays became less fun the closer it came time to return to school, and when we got to the hotel in the hills and my Dad bought us afternoon tea, Jenny and I were close to tears. He tried to cheer us up. Two morose schoolgirls in mufti, jeans and sweatshirts, leg-warmers and ballet pumps, sitting side by side and forcing down cream cakes. Matt was still playing up and we watched the clock, dreading when five thirty came around and the drive through the dark winter evening back to school would begin.

Once back at school, there was only supper and homework to look forward to and then a long, cold winter night in a long, cold dormitory that was filled with the sniffles of those still afflicted by homesickness, the snores of the asthmatics and the cloying scent of twenty pairs of damp woolly tights steaming on the inadequate radiators. I was filled with dreams of kissing Jenny.

It was not until the middle of the summer term that I did kiss her for the first time. The only time. It happening during the school trip to a national park. My sixteenth birthday was looming and I was all sophistication and spots and I sat next to Jenny on the coach.

We sat at the back or as near to it we could. The really naughty girls got the back seat; we didn't go quite that far. So there we were two or three rows forward, Jenny and I, laughing and touching, canoodling, a little like Tony Curtis and Marilyn Monroe but not a lot. The 'One legged jockey' would have left us baffled and we couldn't share each other's lipstick because we hadn't got any. We hadn't even got a handbag with us, not on a field trip. We had to stuff everything into the pockets of our jeans. And there wasn't much room, because we had to make sure we had a couple of obligatory tampons, whether it was time or not. They were essential for scaring the shit out of the unfortunate male teachers who had been press-ganged onto the trip. How those spotty inadequates ended up teaching in an all girls school is totally beyond me. They never stood a chance. We made their lives miseries, we really were quick on the draw with the sanitary products.

We had painted our nails together the night before. Jeans and sweats and clunky hiking boots may have been the order of the day as far as clothing was concerned, but that didn't entirely preclude a bit of glamour, so we'd shared nail varnish, mixed and matched colors, held our wet nails in water to allegedly dry them faster. What did preclude a bit of glamour was one of our more humorless teachers. She primly pointed out that the ban on nail adornments applied even on school trip days and insisted we make us of the remover pronto. We were left just with tell tale pale pink stains on our cuticles.

Once in the fresh air we giggled and strolled, allegedly studying the flora and fauna as we walked through the summer, grey hills.

Mid morning and we found ourselves detached from the rest of the group in a cool, lonely spot. I asked her if I could kiss her. She hesitated and I explained, we'd just be practicing, so it wouldn't look like we were completely hopeless when we came to try it with a boy. She agreed. She wasn't overly enthusiastic but she reluctantly let me kiss her.

We started gently. I could feel the down on her upper lip and the softness of her lovely mouth. I probably also smelt the unspeakable packed lunch we'd just eaten, rank boiled eggs and bloody margarine. If I did, I didn't notice and gently pushed my tongue between her reluctant, pink lips. She didn't respond, perhaps a little bit, but in truth hardly at all. I think I sensed that she wasn't really enjoying herself but I delved deeper with my hesitant tongue. She pulled away. I was breathless but only for a second as I quickly remembered myself and my cover story. "Did I do it right?" We were only supposed to be practicing and comparing notes after all. She didn't say anything.

Do you want to have another go?

No!

Go on.

She looked down and mumbled something. I bent towards her and the tip of our tongues touched. She pulled away and ran up the path. I ran after her, squealing and laughing. We were two gawky schoolgirls in cumbersome hiking boots and too tight jeans stumbling along a rough, uneven track. One of us was bound to fall. It was Jenny. I was always marginally the better athlete. She stumbled and rolled into the long grass at the side of the path. I raced in after her.

Jenny are you alright?

She didn't reply.

I knelt down and looked at her. She wouldn't look at me. I crawled in beside her on the damp grass.

Are you alright?

Just grazed my knees that's all.

Kiss me again. I breathed.

She did, she bloody well did.

There on the side of the path, on a cold and wet typically grey English summer day. We kissed and my hand was soon inside her aertex blouse, seeking out the elusive, budding breast in her over-ambitious bra. She didn't stop me. My other hand went to her crotch. She didn't stop me.

It was the scream of '*rug munchers*' that did.

Two boys from a nasty northern comprehensive school also making a tour of the beautiful Derbyshire landscape to give the kids a break from gritty urban reality and to give the teachers the chance of a doss. The boys stood over us, first formers by the look of them, snotty and jam stained, they merely jeered at us at first but very soon they launched into a far more vicious cacophony:

"Dykes, dykes, dirty fucking dykes."

They were dancing around and shouting, pointing at us and laughing; *"fucking rug munchers, lesbians, lesbos."*

In normal circumstances we could have sorted them out. Jenny definitely could. I might have been the better athlete, but she was by far the better boxer, she had a more aggressive streak. But we just ran down the path. It seemed the simplest solution. The boys didn't follow. We had chosen this secluded spot for, well, you know what; they'd chosen it for a crafty fag. They contented themselves with a massive bawl of "Queers" and lit up.

Once we were out of sight I stopped and pulled Jenny up.

Shall we do it again?

Not bloody likely. I'm not risking that again.

Alright, but later, when we get back, somewhere private.

We'll see.

Say yes.

We'll see.

When we get back?

She said nothing and ran off in search of the main party. I didn't run after her, just sauntered in her wake. Thinking to myself: "When we get back, when we get back, I can't wait."

Jenny was late coming into the dining room for supper that night, so we didn't sit together. She sat far away from me, pensive, refusing to catch my eye. After supper we had to do homework for an hour and a half, so I didn't get a chance to speak to her and then she went straight to her dorm, a dorm I did not share. She was late getting down to breakfast next morning, so once again we didn't sit together and she wouldn't catch my eye. Next it was lessons. At lunchtime I caught her eye and immediately wished I hadn't, her eyes were black, tired and cautious. They were frightened eyes. She looked down and refused to look up again. Finally after lunch I managed to get her alone; she managed to get away from me.

She avoided me for the whole of the next week and for much of the one that followed that and that was not easy in our closed community of erupting spots and swinging hormones.

I had to accept that I would have to find another crush. It was not easy and with my characteristic childish constancy I cried myself to sleep every night for at least a week afterwards. There was one day that was truly hard. It was raining heavily and there was no games that afternoon, which didn't bother me too much because I'd gone off hockey and I never liked lacrosse. Tennis was my sport that year, and the courts were being refurbished, like they were every winter. God, the trials and tribulations of a public school-girl! No tennis because the contractors are in. 'Contractors in'—Is that a euphemism?

But without an activity to take my mind off Jenny I turned to my library book, '*Famine*' by Liam O'Flaherty. It's crushingly sad and just what you need when you are already inclined to be tearful. I put it down and tried to distract myself from thoughts of Jenny. Soon I was in floods of tears, my chest was heaving and I cried like a child. For a few agonized moments I knew that nothing could make things better and a few moments after that things *were* better. It's a tragedy when we lose the ability to cry like a child, the innocent release does so much good. To paraphrase Picasso, 'I've spent my life learning to cry like a child again.'

For all of the reasons above I hung back. I hesitated and left Michelle sitting across the hall from me, two wallflowers. It had been so different earlier in the day, we had such a great time together that I thought that maybe we could go beyond mere friendship, I thought that Michelle might return my feelings.

We'd spent the day together, sauntering around the shops in St Malo, laughing as we tried on straw hats, sitting on the quayside gazing contentedly out to sea, drinking a glass of gut-rot apiece in a quaint little café and giggling nervously as we shrugged off the attentions of a party of slightly seedy men who were old enough to be our fathers and certainly old enough to know what they were suggesting was totally inappropriate. This shared experience brought us together. I thought I learnt something from my earlier encounters with Evie and Jenny, that I could read the signs, that maybe Michelle was the one. That she wouldn't reject me.

I was convincing myself of this as I hesitated on the shabby institutional chair in the sports hall. And whilst I hesitated Michelle was approached by a boy. She smiled at him. She said yes, and soon they were on the dance floor together. She fell prey to his wandering hands, corrupted by his acne and cowed by his evolutionary imperatives. He wrapped himself around her, pawed and pressed her. I turned away and let my regrets wrap themselves around me.

I sat there burning up inside, just as I would the next day as I surreptitiously watched Michelle and her beau cavort on the school bus all the way to Caen and back.

I burnt with might have beens. Might have been with Evie, might have been with Jenny, might have been with Michelle.

Brad Craddock

Brad Craddock teaches creative writing at the School of the Arts in Rochester, NY, and is the author of the comic novels *Alice's Misadventures Underground* and *The Curse of the Dark Woods*. Currently, he writes film reviews for ImageOut and serves on the Board of Directors.

The Mastectomy

At the prick of the needle, the thin
Waves of consciousness swirl before her
Dulling eyes, and just before the sea
Drags her under, she is afloat in the wish
That she had been born a boy.

Perhaps that would not have saved her.
But speculation is as speculation—
Any preserver thrown to preserve her
From this sad and drowning flesh.
Then the dark sinking into deep waters.

When she wakes, she is half herself
And something else, washed ashore.
No more a lure, rather than a trap.
She hears the siren's song—it is the voice
of her sisters waiting for her to swim ashore.

Here's Rosemary and a Little Rue

While other boys flexed their ropey arms
In sports that exerted endless effort
I entertained myself in books.

Therein
I traversed old, dead ruins—their columns broken
Like children's dreams. Harms unspoken
Filled each golden plate set full and heaping for the
Feast.

At least these goblin tomes removed me
For a time from a stark, though burgeoning reality
That I did not love as other boys loved.

I loved their Herculean bodies
I loved their Atalanta grace and strength
I loved their Narcissine beauty
I loved their tragic hubris, that spiral fall of confidence.

And loving, loved them from afar,
As if I put my right hand out
And longing for their human touch, came up
Dissatisfied, in short,
As if their hands were gloved.

I move as shadow in the woods
Lightly touching a past hardly used
For fear of breaking something long,
pointless, and necessary, like my heart.

Avery Johnstone

Avery Johnstone lives in the city of Rochester, NY with his partner and pet rabbit. He is a janitor and genderqueer.

While I Was 'Out'

When I was twenty years old, a girlfriend let me borrow a copy of *Stone Butch Blues* by Leslie Feinberg. Whether she said as much directly or she just implied it (I can't remember), the message was clear—you have a lot in common with the protagonist, Jess. This, along with some other experiences, launched me into a long period of continuous introspection, searching to understand some gender-related questions. I was still grappling with my sexual orientation at that point, and gender identity added yet another dimension. At times they felt so intertwined I couldn't really tell them apart; other times they were so far from each other one seemed to have absolutely nothing to do with the other. Over time, I've found some happy medium somewhere between those two extremes. Gender identity and sexual orientation co-exist and inform each other, but they are also very separate aspects of who a person is.

In some ways, how I have appeared and identified over time is a typical path for someone who is born female and is somewhere on the transmasculine side of things. I was a tomboy who never grew out of that as a phase. I slowly came out to myself as a lesbian. I decided that because of my gender expression, that must mean I'm butch. But I never felt that. I kept searching and searching, and I could not quite find where I fit. I was becoming less sure of the lesbian thing. Maybe I'm attracted to men. Or maybe people of all genders. Was I a transsexual? This term was somewhat common ten years ago, but is already quite outdated. The preferred term is transgender.

Was I meant to transition and live as a man? The pressure to find myself kept leading to dead ends, and I was increasingly freaked beyond belief.

I graduated college, came back home to Rochester, and tried to leave some of that heavy stuff behind. To a large extent, I had just given up and said, "Good enough." I tried to move on and do life as best I could. I tried to get out there, meet people, get involved! I was connecting on personal levels with people, whether that was through a group (I was in the GAGV youth group from 2000-2004, and was in a gender identity group therapy dynamic from 2004-2006), at conferences (I went to a handful between 2004 and 2006), or just hanging out one-on-one and talking about difficult stuff. I did an AIDS walk, I volunteered for ImageOut, I did drag at Muthers.

After a couple of years, even that level of involvement was feeling overwhelming. I slowly found myself disconnecting from most things that were causing me too much anxiety. The LGBT community was definitely on that list, but at the time, I would have shrugged it off and told you, "it's just not that important to who I am."

The break-up was never about interpersonal drama or ideological disagreements. (Although, I did feel some of that—I strongly feel that a facilitator/leader can really make or break a group.) I broke away because it felt too sensitive to be in touch with what was going on, and to connect with others on this identity-based level. For the next 6 or so years, I was living *sort of* as the person I envisioned myself to be. I was not living as a woman. I was not living as a man. But, I was also actively squelching my thoughts and feelings about that; about where I might fit on the gender binary, and about how I might be able to improve my quality of life.

I didn't stop being an activist or community contributor, but I did stop focusing on things that hit too close to home. I immersed myself in other endeavors, such as Food Not Bombs, our local Free School, and benefits to raise money for the Flying Squirrel Community Space, Indymedia, etc. I overextended myself way past the point of burn-out. I've taken huge steps back. I'm currently at a precipice, figuring out what to throw my energies into next, and how to do it differently.

I was not very happy in that life, but I had resigned myself to thinking that this was just how things were for me. I was uncomfortable in my own skin. My anxiety levels were very high, on a normal day. On *every* normal day. I self-injured and shut-down (dissociated) regularly, just to cope with daily life. I forced myself to do so many things, all the time out of fear of sinking into yet another depression if I didn't stay active. I was hyper-vigilant of my internal states and tried to regulate all my emotions—squish and smush them, twist them into something else and rationalize them away. I was aware that I was capable of having a sex drive, but it was so far gone I didn't have the slightest idea of how to coax it back. And I really wanted it back.

It's not like my life was all that stressful! I cannot think of a job that would be any less taxing than mine is. I don't have any dependents. I don't have money concerns, health concerns, family issues…nothing! I have an amazingly supportive partner. My home-life is stable. I have friends who understand me. But something was amiss and I wanted to keep ignoring it.

Bottom-line, trying to unravel whether I should medically and socially transition from female to male was running me raw and ragged, for years and years and years. I had a huge amount of body dysphoria. I felt totally lost a lot of the time (literally and figuratively). But it wasn't going to be about gender. It was going to be about any number of other things, and I was going to spend a lot of time and energy constantly picking all of those other things apart!

I did go through a (fortunately unsuccessful) time period where I said, okay, this *is* about gender. And I found a therapist to talk to about that, specifically. I thought I was headed on a neat and tidy (and extremely difficult) path to finally sort this all out and start testosterone and transition into a visible man. Except, I never actually wanted to *be* a man. It's just that I had backed myself into a corner, and this was my escape plan. Ultimately, there was no way that could have worked. I knew myself too well. I never ended up connecting with the therapist. I never even convinced myself to begin with, and the whole plan just stalled out.

After a few more years, I'm finally starting to get it. I've realized that "transition" does not need to look like one thing in particular, and even if I don't relate with every possible piece of it, I am still trans.

I've been seeing a therapist I very much do connect with, and although she doesn't have any specific expertise with gender issues, she is encouraging and open. That is all I really need. When I said, "I need to try testosterone—a low dose—just to see what it would feel like," she replied, essentially, "So do it!"

I worked through the system to get my hands on a topical testosterone gel, and I've been using it daily for about a year and a half now. The dose is so low that I do not look or sound any different; I don't generally pass as male (and this is exactly where I want to be.) Internally though, it made a world of difference for me, almost instantaneously. Within a matter of days, my general anxiety drastically decreased, and I've come into a new baseline. I feel warm and fuzzy, cozy comfortable, in my skin. I finally feel like myself, essentially. Life is not nearly as overwhelming, and I've been slowly finding my way back to what I feel is important. To me, it feels like these shifts have a whole lot more to do with my mental health than it does with my gender identity, but of course, it's all intertwined. As of now, I plan to be on testosterone for the rest of my life if possible, while minimizing physical changes. I'm taking testosterone toward androgyny. Although,

I'm already androgynous, so I plan to just continue transitioning (outwardly) toward more of the same.

In my late-teens, early-twenties, I was only partly out of the closet, while being very involved in the community. I was not specifically hiding anything, but I wasn't vocal in the least, either. It's easy to not talk about who you are when you rarely talk at all to begin with. And *this, specifically,* is what I've been working on, because my ultimate goal is to feel comfortable as a social person. I don't talk much at all on a daily basis. I have a handful of people who I talk to *a lot.* (Just ask my partner!) Beyond that, I don't talk to people—not about the weather, not about myself, not about local news. I am slowly trying to change this.

So when I say I want to come out, what I mean is that I want to be comfortable talking to any and everyone, to varying degrees, about my life, about what I'm doing, and about my take on who I am. I'm a pro at hearing about this stuff from everyone else, but I have a ways to go. I want to stop filtering. I want to be able to just casually say, "My partner and I did such-and-such this weekend." And actually use her name and her pronouns. In more advanced situations, I want to include more about my gender identity. I started to come out to some family members as non-binary recently, but there's a whole lot more to do.

All along, there's one way I've always been "out," and that's been through my appearance. I never compromise on that—not while growing up (and I was fortunate to have parents who didn't meddle too much), and certainly not now. I appear how I want to appear. I wear what I want to wear. And people can come to assumptions easily based on that. The assumptions are probably pretty far off from how I actually identify (read: butch lesbian—yet, I am so not butch!), but I can live with that. It's much better than feeling uncomfortable with how I look.

In retrospect, I think that the fact I've been so uncomfortable in my body is the reason why I've always given myself a lot of leeway on the things I *can* control: clothing, shoes, accessories, hairstyles. Essentially: gender presentation. I have rarely cared what others think, in terms of the way I look. And I've been fortunate to have never gotten too much flak about it (or, perhaps, I've been oblivious...)

Why do I want to come back to the LGBT (specifically the T) community? Some of the reasons are selfish. I started a very low dose of testosterone, and now the community feels relevant to my life again. But another way to phrase that exact same notion would be, "I've finally found where I belong, in a positive way, and it's within the trans community. Now that I've gotten through the bulk of the personal struggles, I want to give something back." I'm not sure how, exactly, but some pretty safe bets would be: through writing, through connecting personally with others, through local community involvement, and eventually, through being more open and out about who I am on a daily basis.

Mohammad Seraji

Mohammad is one of your friendly baristas at Equal
Grounds Coffeehouse in the Southwedge. Outside of his
work in coffee retail, he is known as Gloria Schaaft the
local celebrated personality drag queen.

Leap Day

You left your camera at my place
so
I'm going to take dirty
pictures of myself
on it for you to
see.

You'll be embarrassed
for me, but I won't be.

In a world where
every four years, we take a day extra,
to account for error
in our calendars,

I would be embarrassed to think
human experience is anything
but random.

You can flip from cover to cover
of the Camera Owner's Manual, clinging to some notion
or ethics and I'm no

goddess or fortune teller, but I know
the answer will not be in writing. For

would we have a word for *purr*
if we did not hear the cats do it
first?

Insanity was Described to Me as Endless Repetition of the Same Action, Expecting to Yield Different Results

When I was a child I
wet a string with my spit
and placed it on an illuminated lightbulb
It exploded, and luckily
no one was hurt, but I never
tried that one again.

No matter how many times you throw yourself
into me, we will not converge into one.
No two-headed manbeasts
roam this earth; the pictures
you draw me are largely based on
Television dramas, Neolithic
cave paintings, why try,
each night, to assume these positions, in the hours so
dark, magic
can defend its existence.

In the morning you'll take me to the river and bathe me
while I am sleeping; I do not stir.
Your patience shorter than my
persistence to continue dreaming, you leave me, angry
or
discouraged.

I don't mind waking up here alone, when the water is
warm
in the autumn.

Once I followed the river
down past the marshes at the very end
of the tributaries—I found myself at the beginning
of an even larger body
of water.

Drew Payne

Drew is a writer living in London, UK. His work has appeared in *Chroma, Velvet Mafia, Creative Week, Out in the City* and *ImageOutWrite, volume 1*. He writes regularly for *Nursing Standard* and *NRC* magazines, and he has written and performed sketches in the *Treason Show*, a Brighton based satirical review show.

The Third Option

Evening

The flat was already warm when I walked in, hot air pushing against the cold skin of my face as soon as I opened the front door. We had our neighbors to thank for this, not the central heating system we only carefully used because of its high cost. The building we live in has a large number of small flats squeezed into its structure. We can often hear our neighbors through the thin walls but we also get the heat from their heating systems pouring through them too. That evening I was more than grateful for it.

My body was aching from the frustrations of the day and the weather had turned icy cold now the rain had stopped. The warmth of our home was reassuring, as reassuring as simply being back in our home.

I left my coat and bag in the tiny hallway, and went straight into our bedroom. There I stripped off my work clothes, dropping them on our bed, and made my way into our tiny bathroom, which is actually off our bedroom. I wanted a shower, the water to wash away the tiredness in my body, but more so.

The hot water did ease some of those aches, washing over my body, but it also gave me a handful of minutes where I didn't have to think. I could just stand there and let the shower perform the work. Instead, today my mind was rushing with thoughts, uncomfortable thoughts and questions, and it wouldn't even rest for a moment in the shower.

After I'd dried myself, I pulled on a sweat shirt and a pair of sweat pants. Then I moved into our sitting room, put the television on and dropped down onto our sofa. The evening news was on and I just let its stories of tragedy and political depression wash over me. My mood still felt uncomfortable and disturbed.

I'd thought my life here with Dan had been happy but now I doubted it. We had each other, but everything else seemed so hard. We were always short of money. We had to save what little spare cash for anything extra we wanted, or we went without it, the latter happening most times. Our home, a housing association flat Dan had secured when he first came here, was tiny. We both fit into it, but there never seemed any space to spare. My career had stalled with my current job. I thought it would be an avenue to promotion, instead I was stuck at the same grade and there was no hope of any promotion, especially with my incompetent manager. Dan still enjoyed his job but he was hopelessly underpaid. Even with Dan in my life, my family was still maintaining a very chilly relationship with me. This wasn't the life I had envisioned for myself, even with

Dan there, and tonight the feeling of disappointment lay heavily on me. My life felt like such a failure and so soon.

To my surprise the news program finished. I barely remembered any of the items from it. It was replaced with a fluffy chat show. My mind was even less inclined to watch this. As I started to push myself off the sofa, I heard the flat's front door open. It had to be Dan.

Dan, wrapped up in his old coat, was still wearing his work clothes, and looked at me in surprise as I rushed up to him. Without saying anything, I threw my arms around him and drew our bodies together in a tight embrace. His body was cold from the outside air, but he was still so deeply reassuring. He smelt of his work: of fresh timber and sweat. I nestled my face into his neck as his own arms quickly unfolded around me.

"You okay?" Dan asked me.

"I just wanted a hug," I replied, my face still pressed into his neck.

"You jump me for a hug before I can even get my coat off."

"Sorry," I mumbled.

"You had a bad day?" Dan asked.

"Yes."

Dan kissed me on the top of my head, then ran his hand down the side of my face, his calloused fingers stroking over my skin.

"Let me have a shower and then we can talk," he said.

"Sorry," I replied, suddenly feeling embarrassed by my own need.

"Don't be. That's why I'm here. But let me get out of my work clothes. I stink."

"Yes," I said as we disentangled ourselves from our embrace.

Lunchtime

I hurried along the street, keeping close to the shop fronts and trying to avoid the cold, heavy rain. I only had thirty minutes to get my lunch before my next client interview and I was rushing. I was concentrating on my route and not on those around me, so when I heard Jerry's voice I almost tripped over with surprise.

"Gabriel!" He called out, using my full name and making me cringe inside. No matter how many times I repeated it, he seemed incapable of calling me Gabe, as everyone else did.

I looked up to see him, under a large golfing umbrella, bearing down upon me.

Jerry worked in the council's accounts office, in the adjacent office to where I worked and since I'd first meet him he seemed to have made it his mission to "save" me. Like water running off the preverbal duck's back, Jerry ignored all my polite attempts to turn him down. He seemed incapable of hearing a rejection to his requests.

"I'm sorry but I'm in a hurry," I replied and tried to rush around him. But Jerry is as big as he is solid in his own views. His tall frame is swathed in rolls of flesh, and he's not the easiest of people to push around.

"You're never too busy to think about where you're going to spend eternity," he bounced back, his body blocking me back against a shop front.

"My church is having a special Save the Homosexual mission this month."

"That's nice," I muttered as I tried to push around him, but he moved into my path, blocking me.

"You must come along," he boomed.

"What?" I replied.

"God never wanted anybody to be homosexual and he can free you from that sterile lifestyle you've chosen," Jerry said, firing his words out at me in a bright rapid stream.

"What?" I again replied, though this time I could feel my checks reddening with embarrassment. I'd been careful not to tell Jerry anything about my relationship with Dan, I'd been careful to tell Jerry as few pieces of information about my life as possible.

"You have chosen the homosexual lifestyle but God does not want you living that sterile and dead lifestyle. God wants you to be happy and whole and God can give you that, Gabriel. All you have to do is give your heart to him," again Jerry fired his words at me, so fast I could barely interrupt him.

"I am happy," I snapped back.

"No you're not," Jerry replied. "God can see into your heart and knows how unhappy you are in this homosexual lifestyle, but he can free you from it. Just come to my church and you will meet God and he will change your life. God will make you happy and free you from the homosexual lifestyle."

"Leave me alone!" I now shouted at him, at the same moment I stepped right out into the street, ignoring the rain, and physically pushing past Jerry.

"Don't harden your heart to God. He has told me that he can free you from your unhappy and unfulfilled lifestyle."

"Get out of my way!" I shouted again as I finally pushed past him and rushed into the sandwich shop next door.

There was a queue in the shop. Not meeting any of the eyes watching me, I simply joined the end of the queue. For a long moment I stood there, my heart pounding in my chest, fearing that Jerry would follow me. But, by the time the third person ahead of me had been served and Jerry had still not entered the shop, I felt my nerves easing. Jerry had given up on me, for the time being at least.

As I waited to be served, I twisted around the ring I wear on my left ring finger. It's a simple, stainless steel band, all we could afford. Dan has a matching one and he calls them our engagement rings. We want to be married but so far all we can afford are these rings, everything else is so expensive and still out of our reach.

Afternoon

I found it hard to concentrate on my work that afternoon. Jerry's words had been pitifully inept. They were never going to make me convert to his religion, but they had rubbed a raw nerve in my mind, and now I couldn't rest.

My parents had the same beliefs as Jerry, except with my father there was no negotiation, and I'd been raised in a very strict Christian home. As a child, I'd made no waves, just believed what I was told. The crisis had come when I was a teenager and I first fell in love, with Karl, who ran the church's Youth Fellowship. I kept my feelings secret at first, but in the end it had come down to a choice between my sexuality and my beliefs, between my true self and Christian self. I chose what was real for me, my sexuality. That choice though caused my family and what felt like my whole life to be wrenched away from me. I had to leave home to be myself.

In Jerry's pitiful words I'd hear echoes of the condemnation my father had poured down on me when he'd finally found out about me.

Now, my mind kept going over and over Jerry's words, and the more I did, the more I began to wonder if there really was any truth in them. My life was not a success. Dan and I were always short of money and only barely manage to get by. We couldn't even save up enough to quietly get married, now that it was finally legal.

Were they right? Was my life sterile and useless? It felt as if my life was on hold. I was merely treading water and not living any sort of fulfilled lifestyle.

When I first left home, before I met Dan, I suffered from severe depression. I had nightmares that I was being condemned to hell; when I was awake I was plagued with doubts. I kept questioning if I'd done the right thing and were those Christians right? Was my life wrong because of my sexuality? Now, as I stared at the paperwork scattered across my desk at work, I could feel those thoughts and doubts, that sinking depression creeping back. It was a cold and frightening feeling.

Evening

Dan was cooking our evening meal. He stood at the kitchen counter, his back bent forward, his hands quickly and nimbly chopping, the sharp knife sliding quickly through the vegetables' flesh, the blade getting nearer and nearer but never harming his own fingers. I sat at the tiny kitchen table and watched him. Dan loves to cook. Even to prepare the simplest meal gives him pleasure. Tonight he was cooking pasta and bolognese, though he was cooking the sauce from scratch. He was preparing the vegetables and mincing the meat to add to the tomato sauce made from tinned tomatoes and onions simmering on the cooker.

He's a carpenter by trade. Working with his hands fulfills him. He spends his working days making wooden furniture, and when he comes home he cooks our meals. Most of the furniture in our home, including our big and solid bed, he has made.

His emotions are as solid as the furniture he makes. He has always said that he doesn't see the point of believing in something that doesn't lift up people. He can't see the point of following a religion that pulls someone down with guilt and a long list of prohibited actions and thoughts.

We talked about this early that evening. Dan had his shower and joined me on the sofa, dressed in jeans and a tee shirt, and without a word, wrapped his arms around me. In reply I buried myself into that hug, suddenly secure again in his embrace. I pushed my face into his neck and he in turn kissed me on the forehead and slowly began to stroke my hair. We stayed silent like that for a long and comfortable moment.

Finally Dan asked me, "What happened today?"

Like a cupboard door opening and its messy contents tumbling out, I opened my mouth and the events of that day fell from me. I told him about my encounter with Jerry, but I also told him about the doubts and low mood that had plagued my whole afternoon.

When I had finished, my words finally drying up, Dan continued to stroke my hair and quietly said, "You always feel things more than I do. That's just you. There's nothing wrong with that and I love that about you."

"I'm sorry," I mumbled in reply.

"Don't worry about it. And don't worry about what that Jerry said. God, what a dick."

"Yes," I replied.

"I've always felt that if you're going to believe in something then it should be something that lifts up people, that is there to help people and make things better. Not something that wraps people up in so many things that they feel guilt ridden and screwed up. God, what's the point of that?"

I could have told him a hundred reasons why people wanted to do that to others, but to Dan we are on this earth to make it a better place in whatever way we can.

"But the money. We've never got enough. We've got to save up for everything. I don't know if we'll ever afford to get married," I said.

"I don't care. So we're not rich, so what? We'll get married one day, but even if we're not married, we've got each other. That's what important to me. You, and being with you. You make me so happy."

Dan's arms pulled me close to him and again I nestled my face in his neck.

I looked up from the kitchen table and saw Dan finished with his preparations. He stood in front of the cooker, where he was juggling three different pans. One had the boiling tomato sauce, one in which the pasta was coming to the boil and in the third, he had begun to fry the vegetables and minced meat. His feet were unmoving. He stood in the same spot, while his upper body bounced around with a lively energy as he tended to those pans. A strand of his fringe kept falling into his eyes. He was so alive when he was making something.

"Thank you," I quietly said.

"What was that?" Dan said, glancing back at me over his shoulder, again tossing the strand of hair out of his eyes.

"Thanks for cooking dinner," I quickly replied.

"No problem," Dan said.

Night

Dan was asleep. He was lying on his side, his face turned towards me, his mouth slightly open, breathing in a slow and rhythmical way. Even in sleep he seemed so relaxed and calm, though his fringe was still falling into his closed eyes.

He'd fallen asleep soon after we'd climbed into bed together. But not me. Our bed is so comfortable, a firm mattress on a solid wooden frame, but the thing that makes it so comfortable and relaxing is sleeping there with Dan. Just his body there in bed with me has always given me a deep comfort. Since we have been living together I hadn't been plagued with nightmares and bad nights where sleep was difficult to find. I no longer saw going to bed as a chore, trying to find sleep. Instead I curl up next to Dan and drift off into a gentle sleep.

That night, still awake, my mind was slowing down from all the thoughts that had been racing through it that night.

I looked over at Dan and as I did, the realization slipped into my mind. I didn't need to worry about needing to be happy. All that nonsense about needing to be a success! Dan loved me and wrapped me up in all the security I needed. I was secure in Dan's love, and that made me so happy.

I pressed my body close to his, rested my head on his chest, feeling the warmth of his body. In reply

Dan muttered something in his sleep and folded his arm around me.

Quinn Powell Gifford

Quinn is a student at the University of Texas at Austin in the Humanities Honors Program. Her focus is the study of folk tales and fairy tales and their interaction with the LGBTQ community. She is a food writer and a poet, and lives with her wife in Austin.

Queen of Hearts

Dad shakes a martini
Mom tinkers in the kitchen
pretending she doesn't hear him.

We're not sneaking out tonight
these are my favorite nights
the ones when I'm enough.

Night looks good on you
moonlit skin crashes into my breath
but I daren't lean in.

You fought with your boyfriend today
what did you tell him
when he asked about you and me?

Bride-to-(never)-be

Inspired by *Untitled, 1969*, by Mary Corse (acrylic with reflecting crystals on canvas)

The day you died I took to the woods,
crashing and tearing like a beast afire
every branch a sacrificial sickle
exsanguinating the despair.

I tore into your room in a rapturous rage,
threw open the wardrobe like a rapacious brigand
only to fall, weeping, at the phantom feet
of your stiff, pristine wedding dress.

I clutched at the fabric until I heard myself screaming,
ripping, stabbing, flaying the very jewels off its surface
'til all at once I awoke, in a pile of textile
a rather different kind of murder scene.

Creeping slow from a nearby window
a honey dawn on the stone floor
illuminating, no, *crystallizing* my tears onto the virgin silk
until the room was drenched in a diamond light.

I took wood, canvas, needle, thread, and began to mend
my heart, and the memory of your lips on my lips
with every stretch, every stitch, you flowed back into me

your ghost a masterpiece reflecting the horizon.
Now the redemptive reparation adorns a wall in
another world,
the solemn soliloquy of two princesses in love.

Rapunzel's Brother

I am the one the storytellers forgot
Locked up alone and quite left to rot.
My tower as high, my window as small
My prince just as handsome, though not quite so
    tall.

Rapunzel, my sister, gets all the attention
Toothsome and famous and full of pretension.
Innocent, you say? A victim, at least?
I'm here to tell you, she's both beauty and beast.

A raffish young man of sixteen was I
With thick, primrose hair and foresty eyes.
I flirted and flattered to ensure my disguise,
My penchant for husbands, not so much for wives.

But my carefree endeavors were short lived at best
My flattery worked, the Faerie Queen was obsessed!
If you've met her you know, one dare not protest,
She gets what she wants, to that I attest!

I dodged her advances, with my best Artemis,
But how she persisted, no one could resist!
So I ran away, under cover of night,
The sea in my mind, the stars as my guides.

I didn't get far, 'til her forces surrounded
Dragged me back to the palace, my courage
  impounded.
"LOCK HIM UP," she exclaimed, in rage and in ire,
"If I can't have him, no other may either!"

So thus I was taken, to a tower and left,
Alone but for a window, a guard and regret,
But wouldn't you know, a silver lining drew near,
The guard was a looker, and entirely queer!

My sister knows well, how romance can billow,
Through a cold tower-room with a moon at the
  window!
Not so long after, one late winter's eve,
My love stole me away, upon his ivory steed.

Now, Dear Reader, you know, a different side of the
  tale
Of our (ig)noble family, all the salacious details
Nevermore will you say, you don't know the way
To live happily ever after...and gay!

Steven Farrington

Steven Farrington is a language professor at Monroe Community College in Rochester, NY. He has taken many language and writing classes over the years, has traveled extensively in Europe and Latin America, and lives in Rochester with his husband, Rick.

Nicola and the Coliseum

He was 59 years old, and Nicola Vitangeli had never been anywhere. Not to Boston to see his cousin Maria, not to Brooklyn where his parents had first landed when they came to this country, and nowhere further east than the Adirondacks as a middle-school boy scout. He had certainly never seen Rome, or as his grandfather used to call it, "Roma, la città eterna." Rome may be an eternal city, he thought, but Nicola knew that his own days were numbered, so he'd better act quickly if he hoped to get over there at long last. He had found almost enough loose change to do so.

Despite his lack of travel, Nicola had just spent about half an hour contemplating the Coliseum. He had been cleaning this very classroom for forty years, and the "new" Italian teacher, Miss Filipetti, had put up this poster when she'd moved in just over seven years ago. It had taken the janitor about three years to work up the courage to say "ciao," and, after a few more months, to ask for some Italian-language worksheets to do at home in his cramped one-bedroom apartment.

The unfortunately-named Nicola was painfully, almost embarrassingly, shy. His mother Carla had always blamed the fact that Salvatore, his *nonno,* or grandfather, had insisted on naming her only son after a favorite, deceased, uncle, while not realizing that in this silly new country, Nicola sounded like a girl's name. Anglo schoolchildren in the 1950's neither knew nor cared that many great Italian men had carried this name with pride, and that this was just an old-country version of Nicholas. Nicola's feeble attempts to be known as 'Nick' had been quickly and easily overpowered by Scott Hamilton, the most persistent of his bullies, who had quickly moved to calling him "Nicoletta," "Nicole," or a whole host of anti-Italian and homophobic slurs. By middle school, his tormentors had invented new ways of humiliating the scrawny lad with dark, sad eyes and a swarthy, Mediterranean complexion. They stuck gum in his curly brown hair, and even taken to holding him upside-down in the boy's toilet. These "swirlies" as they were known abated somewhat, along with the "wedgies" and other means of torture, only toward the end of high school as the boys slowly matured and, one by one, got girlfriends.

Nicola only had kid sisters and a perpetually drunk father who worked the night shift at Kodak, so there was no one to stand up for him. By sophomore year, the damage was done. He hadn't even attended his own junior prom when he dropped out. He only attended one dance, a homecoming event held in the fall of his junior year, where he had stood to the side, alone, an awkward and silent wallflower. Toward the end of the night, when no girl had invited him to dance, he quietly snuck out and drove home without anyone noticing, not even Mrs. Chase, the math teacher who was the most observant of the chaperones.

Nicola always left the boys' bathroom for last, cleaning it sometimes as late as five-thirty in the morning. Even after all these years, he could barely stand to be in that place.

Nicola's *nonno,* the old man who had basically raised him and his sisters after their mother had died in a car crash in 1959, used to see evidence of the bullying that Nicola endured. The boy grew adept at concealing every bruise and scrape, but could not hide everything from the observant old man. Salvatore tried to enroll his grandson in boxing classes, but Nicola had been too much of a "wimp" or a "pansy," according to the trainers, to be any good. Just like almost everything else he tried, Nicola had been a dismal failure, and used to skip boxing class to go instead to the movies. The boy soon retreated in a secret world of glamorous Hollywood ladies and their handsome leading men. He especially liked Liz Taylor. He secretly knew that Liz would be his friend, possibly his only friend, if only he could meet her. He was fascinated by her role in *Suddenly, Last Summer,* and he was mesmerized by her violet eyes, her sensuality and savoir-faire. He didn't know to express it yet, but he was also fascinated with Montgomery Clift, but for very different reasons. Years later, when *Cleopatra* came out, Nicola saw the film a total of nine times. He loved the opulent sets and numerous costume-changers his diva made throughout the film, and the only time he put any weight on his meager frame was thanks to too much popcorn at the cinema that summer of 1963.

Inspired by the acting of Audrey Hepburn, Nicola had gone to see a repeat showing of the movie featuring her and Gregory Peck, *Roman Holiday*. When Nicola saw Princess Ann, played by Hepburn, meet the handsome Joe Bradley at Rome's Spanish Steps, he knew he would have to travel one day to that magical city and see it for himself.

When he was all alone in the dark cinema, Nicola felt like no one could hurt him, no one could judge him, and no one even would know where to find him. Years later, when he was arrested in a movie theatre, Nicola felt betrayed by the one place he'd once thought of his refuge.

After his arrest, Nicola had begun going to baseball games. He supported the Red Wings, a local minor-league team whose stadium he could reach by foot from his apartment. Even though he'd never been good at sports, and kids had always teased that he "threw like a girl," in gym class, Nicola eventually developed a true love for the game and an appreciation for the players, whose careers and personal lives he followed obsessively through the years as each man progressed from the minor leagues to the majors, usually after stopping for a while to play with the Minnesota Twins. Nicola even kept dozens of scrapbooks in which he recorded stats, photos, and newspaper clippings about every game he saw and listened to on the radio.

He enjoyed drinking beer until his vision blurred at those games and crunching the shells of his salty peanuts under his feet as he watched the game, savoring the fresh air and the drunken escape that such outings gave him. He would usually walk home in a fog of a beer-buzz, almost daring someone to jump him as he did so, as he lived in kind of a bad neighborhood. Sometimes, fellow fans leaving the stadium gave him a ride, and he loved it if it was a group of good-looking guys. When this happened, he finally felt the acceptance from other men that he had craved for so many years. Following baseball had given Nicola a much-needed hobby and even a sense of camaraderie with his fellow fans, something he had never felt before.

Since the age of twelve, or perhaps even before, Nicola had always known he was different. His *nonno* had said it was because he had the heart of a poet, like Dante, whose verses he sometimes read to him at night, and his mother had even whispered that she would be pleased if her son became a priest, even if it meant no one to pass on the family name. But by the time of his early-onset puberty, Nicola knew the real reason. This was why he never complained about the bullying at school and why he spent long hours praying to the Madonna at Our Lady of Lourdes Church. He was cursed, and he knew it. By the time he was in his mid-thirties, Nicola had given up hope that he could be normal, but he still asked God for forgiveness and offered a vague confession to father Ruggiero each time he screwed up.

Nicola hadn't even been good at being a homosexual. At first, he had tried going to the parks and truck stops, but after his movie-house arrest, he'd never been able to seek public sex again. There had been a time when he had frequented the baths, but that, too, had run its course. Now he called up a gentleman named Chris once a month for a "body rub" that sometimes included a "happy ending," although less and less often than before. Chris was a personal trainer who still looked amazing although he was now almost middle-aged. He had explained, back when he was still in college, that he couldn't advertise as a "massage therapist" as he didn't have the required credentials. Nicola had been glad to help the younger man pay for college on his meager janitor's salary and, after his three cats and his one remaining sister, Chris was the closest thing Nicola had ever had to a friend.

"Do you think you'll ever get a boyfriend?" Chris had asked once, brushing a blond lock of hair back over his handsome face which was lit up by beautiful blue eyes.

"No," Nicola had said after thinking about it for a moment. "No. I don't deserve one."

"Oh, come on," Chris said, crooking an elbow under his beautifully-cleft chin and smiling at his long-term client. "Come on, buddy. Everybody deserves to have some love in their life."

"Not me," Nicola said, looking past Chris at the locked cabinet where he kept all his VCR tapes. Hal at the video store had suggested he upgrade to that new invention, the DVD, but Nicola had preferred to stick to the machine he knew how to operate. He figured he had enough tapes and magazines of vintage gay porn to last him to the end of his life if necessary.

"So," said Chris, sitting up in bed and trying a new tactic, "you must have been in the army or something. Most guys your age went to Vietnam. Did you go? I bet *that* would've been a great way to meet guys," Chris said with the self-assurance of those who have never really suffered or had to work for anything.

"I wanted to go," Nicola said slowly, realizing he had never told anyone, not even Father Ruggiero, what he was about to tell the young man. "I wanted to go. I wanted to die over there. I hoped to get blown to smithereens because killing yourself is a mortal sin. And I didn't want to burn in Hell. So, my plan was to die over there. All the way the hell in Asia. Hell, I've never even left New York State. But they rejected me."

"Shit," Chris said, looking genuinely sorry.

"Shit is right," Nicola said. "I got rejected 'cause of my damn asthma and my crappy eyes."

"Wow, Chris said, reaching over to take Nicola's hand for the first time after ten years of body contact. "So what happened instead?"

To this, Nicola just chuckled. "You're lookin' at it." Nicola took a swig from the can of Genesee beer he had brought out for the special occasion that Chris's visits always were. He took a long look at the young man, trying to decide whether or not to continue telling his story. Chris looked at him as if he wanted him to go on, so he did.

"I had to get out of my house. I needed a job. One that a shy, barely-literate person could do. I did spend one summer flipping burgers at Schaller's, but then I became a janitor in Greece, in the same school where I used to get bullied as a kid." He stopped, studying Chris's reactions. "I know, kinda pathetic."

Chris seemed to ignore this last comment. "It's actually funny," he said with a thoughtful smile. "They call it the Town of Greece, and you're Italian."

"Yeah," Nicola said. "My grandpa was a proud Roman, but he'd always wanted to go to Greece. So, when they arrived in Rochester in the 40's, that's where a lot of Italians lived. On the working-class West Side. So, that's where I grew up, and that's where I still work. Hey, only two bus rides away most nights," he said, watching Chris slipping on his sexy, slightly-ripped jeans.

As Nicola reached for his wallet, Chris reached out his hand for the second time and said, "This time's on the house, buddy. Merry Christmas."

The next day, Nicola sat quietly and ill-at-ease in the midst of a living room full of wrapping-paper, his nephews playing something called Resident Evil on something called a PlayStation. Nicola wondered if he had indirectly paid for this silliness, as all his extra cash went to his sister. While Rita argued with her jerk of a husband in the kitchen, and the pasta boiled on the stove, Nicola closed his eyes and smiled as he thought of Chris and how that conversation the night before had probably been the longest one of his entire life, and the most fulfilling.

Nicola slowly chewed his cold eggplant-parmesan sub while working on tonight's Italian "homework." Miss

Filipetti had always been kind enough to grade his papers, in green pen no less, and his grades had been steadily improving. He was now in the equivalent of third-year Italian, and Miss Filipetti had left him a kind note stating that she wanted him to try a Regent's Exam, which Nicola had heard of, but had never taken himself while in school, as he had not been deemed "college material" back in the day. She had even once written on a post-it note that he was her "best student," which Nicola assumed at first was a joke. After he decided that maybe it wasn't, he'd framed the note and kept it on his wall at home, out of reach of the cats, all of whom were strays who had presented themselves randomly on his doorstep. Nicola never really went out of his way to get anything good in life- he felt that he didn't deserve it, after all- but when God gave him something randomly, like a cat, or loose change, who was he to turn it down?

It had been about six years ago, shortly after the new millennium, when Nicola had gotten the idea of putting money aside-only money that he found at school-for his trip, the one that would finally take him to Rome.

He'd actually calculated the average amount of change he found per week a few times. The average varied in surprising ways, but it generally hovered around three dollars per week. Nicola kept it all in neatly-rolled stacks in his closet. This week had been pretty good so far-one dollar bill, crinkled but in acceptable shape, and $3.60 in loose change. He now had nearly a thousand dollars. He hadn't contacted a travel-agent yet, but Chris had assured him that this would surely cover a plane ticket as well as a modest hotel-room. This year, at the end of August, after summer school ended but before Labor Day, if God willed it, Nicola would take his first vacation ever. He hadn't ever taken a sick day or vacation time, but now he would let the Ukrainian family that cleaned the elementary school cover for him for once.

As Nicola gazed upon the Coliseum poster again, the one showing the grand structure his *nonno* had assured him had been built by their ancestors, he sincerely hoped that the slight pain he felt in his stomach was only a pang of excitement or hope. These were new feelings for Nicola, and it seemed perfectly logical that he should have some physiological response. The fact that his *nonno* had died of stomach cancer and his father of liver failure didn't daunt Nicola, at least not tonight, not while gazing at the Coliseum. His gaze drifted to a new poster Miss Filipetti had hung up, this one a poster for Barilla pasta. The poster featured a smiling young man with dark and beautiful eyes, very white teeth, and just a wisp of day-old stubble on his chin that Nicola found alluring.

Nicola had never been to the doctor as an adult, and he wasn't about to start now. If he could make it just a few more months, get to Rome, and maybe meet a nice Italian man like the one in the poster who would drive him around on his Vespa.... Well then, that would be enough. He could just lay his head down on the banks of the Tiber River, or *il Tevere*, and die a happy man.

A slight smile still on his lips, Nicola looked down at his worksheet again. Tonight's assignment was on the subjunctive mood, which was, as the worksheet explained, most definitely *not* a tense. Nicola read over the sheet, and his eye rested on a verb: aspettare. Nicola couldn't quite remember if it meant "to hope" or perhaps "to wait."

He decided to walk over to the dictionary on the shelf to look it up.

Christine Noble

A political scientist by training and poet at heart,
Christine Noble lives in Rochester, NY. She is the author
of two collections of poetry, *Ego Codex* and *Drawing
Lines*.

Victoria and Adam

There was a monster
living deep inside
an unthinkable beast
the villagers would put to the flame
so what was I to do
but create a new one
something to distract
something to draw their ire
and admiration

I stitched him together
from instructions
I saw on television
knowing what it took to hide the other
the one pointed out to me
by Jodi Foster and Ted Levine

I wore the new monster
like a grotesque mask
hiding my real monster
beneath a skin of anger
of eager jock sniffing
and aggressive punk affectations

This monster held the other at bay
for twenty years and a few days
it held everything else away as well
peace
love
understanding
It did its job with vigor
and not a lick of examination

It crashed over the landscape
of a scared and scarred soul
crashing through the lives
of the innocent and unwary
leaving a trail of smoking ruins
relationships crumbling
security wanting

Then the unthinkable happened
the real beast broke free
tip toeing carefully into the world
still frightened from years of prison
creating worlds of new havoc
It was funny though
she was not as bad as I thought
a bit larger than life
and a bit hard to swallow
but I realized that was everyone else
not me

I learned to love her
the real monster
that was not a monster at all
and while the other still roams
from time to time

he is finding his place
next to her
of her
and within me

IMAGEOUT

In 1993, the Rochester Lesbian & Gay Film & Video Festival was established under the auspices of The Gay Alliance of the Genesee Valley and The Rochester Lesbian and Gay Political Caucus. The first festival included 18 programs and 100 films or videos and focused upon celebrating and documenting the past and present of the global Lesbian and Gay community. Each show attracting almost 90% of the theatre's capacity so the festival founders knew they started a vital and exciting community event. The Rochester LGBT community had received their first taste of what would become the largest annual cultural event in our community.

By 1995, the Film Festival had grown dramatically. More than 100 films and videos were exhibited and the first closing night gala reception at the George Eastman House Museum became an annual celebratory conclusion to the festival week. Archival Night at the Dryden Theatre was also introduced in 1995, featuring classic films of gay cinema's past from the George Eastman House Museum Motion Picture Archives. A third venue, The University of Rochester, allowed the Festival to reach a younger audience. An enthusiastic and diverse audience of more than 4,000 pressed to attend often sold out films.

As a result of such rapid growth and support, the Rochester Lesbian & Gay Film & Video Festival successfully incorporated in 1996 as an independent, not-for-profit 501(c) 3 corporation and the festival was named ImageOut. After four years, ImageOut joined the ranks of the ever-growing national Lesbian and Gay Film Festival community, rivaling many festivals in cities both comparable to and larger than Rochester.

Celebrating its 20th year in 2012 with the first *ImageOutWrite* collection of 23 contemporary writers (available online and at Imageout.org), ImageOut, a community-based volunteer organization, continues to attract local, national and international artists, filmmakers, writers, and a diverse viewing audience. It has served as a major vehicle in promoting lesbian, gay, bisexual, and transgender visibility and an understanding of our lives.